THE PRIESTHOOD
OF *ALL* BELIEVERS

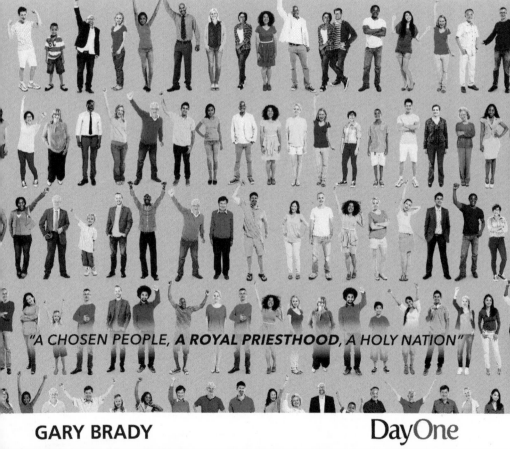

"A CHOSEN PEOPLE, A ROYAL PRIESTHOOD, A HOLY NATION"

GARY BRADY

*Day*One

© Day One Publications 2023

ISBN 978-1-84625-751-3

Unless otherwise indicated Scripture quotations in this publication are from
The Holy Bible, New International Version (NIV),
© 1973, 1978, 1984, 2011
by Biblica, Inc. All rights reserved.

British Library Cataloguing in Publication Data available

Published by Day One Publications
Telephone 01568 613 740
Toll Free 888 329 6630 (North America)
email—sales@dayone.co.uk
web site—www.dayone.co.uk

Printed by 4edge Limited

This book is dedicated, appropriately enough,
to the Priest family—
to my deacon Paul, to Philippa
and to Jonathan, Reuben and Lilly!

4 The priesthood of all believers

It may startle us to learn that every Christian is a priest. But, as Gary Brady shows, the priesthood of all believers glorifies Christ, our great High Priest, and liberates God's children to live all of life for God's glory. Brady's treatment of this precious subject is enlightening, refreshing, and practical. Highly recommended!"

Dr Joel R. Beeke
President, Puritan Reformed Theological Seminary
Grand Rapids, Michigan, USA

Our understanding of what it means to be a Christian is all too often blinkered. We home in on our being born again, justified, and assured of an everlasting home in heaven; yet manage to overlook the plethora of other dimensions of salvation. In these pages, Gary Brady very helpfully leads us though one in particular: the fact we belong to a unique priesthood along with all true believers. It is an aspect of our new life in Christ that opens up a whole new horizon on what it means to live for Christ in the church and in the world. Anyone who reads this volume is guaranteed to be both surprised and challenged by what this means for us in our daily life of faith and service.

Mark G. Johnston
Groomsport Evangelical Presbyterian Church
Northern Ireland

Gary Brady presents a wonderful but often-neglected truth in a clear and helpful way. He uses interesting illustrations and inserts to explore changing ideas of priesthood throughout church history, and outlines the role of priests in the Old and New Covenants. This book is Christ-centred and practical, focusing on how all believers can live out their priesthood today in every aspect of life and particularly through holiness, faith, praise, Bible-reading, prayer, intercession and sharing, looking forward to the day when we will serve Christ perfectly face-to-face.

Elizabeth El Mostain
Pastor's wife and author of 'Survival Tips for Mums'
France

Commendations

The priesthood of all believers? Don't think that this subject doesn't matter. It does. Very much. With both his Bible and his history book open Gary Brady will explain to you the what and the why, and a good deal else. And all in 80 pages! Your whole Christian life could be changed by the end of the week.

Stuart Olyott
Preacher and conference speaker
North Wales

I am very happy to commend Gary Brady's little book on a subject that has often received too little attention among Christians. In a clear and informative way, he demonstrates its importance and indicates how unbiblical is any form of priestcraft now that Jesus has become our high priest and the one mediator between God and human beings. At the same time, it is full of encouragements to apply the truth to our daily lives and to look forward to the priestly service of all believers in the world to come.

Philip H. Eveson
former Principal of the London Seminary
Wrexham, N. Wales

The doctrine of the priesthood of believers is sadly neglected today, and yet it is such an important, edifying, and practical theme. This little book is a valuable resource, including much good material in short compass. You will be informed, encouraged, and challenged as you read.

Bill James
Principal, London Seminary

Contents

Acknowledgements

Whenever one writes a book, one incurs a debt to many others. First and foremost, there is my wife Eleri. Further, there is the ever changing congregation at Childs Hill where these chapters first saw the light of day as a short series of sermons.

Then there are friends in the ministry. I was particularly helped by a discussion of the subject at the Westminster ministers' fellowship here in London.

I mention some of the books that I have perused in the introduction. I have also benefited from a number of articles found online that also address the subject.

Lastly, there are the folk at Day One who have been such a help seeing this publication through to the point where it is now in your hands. Thank you for giving it your attention.

Introduction

'I do not need any earthly priest to mediate between my heavenly Father and me. I have the privilege to draw near to him directly through Jesus Christ' (Craig Troxel).

On that day HOLY TO THE LORD will be inscribed on the bells of the horses, and the cooking pots in the LORD's house will be like the sacred bowls in front of the altar. Every pot in Jerusalem and Judah will be holy to the LORD Almighty, and all who come to sacrifice will take some of the pots and cook in them.

Zechariah 14:20–21

It was many, many years ago, when I was still a young man, that I heard a sermon on the text Zechariah 14:20–21. The phrase HOLY TO THE LORD was inscribed on the gold plate that the High Priest wore on his head. Around the hem of his sacred garment he would have bells that would tinkle as he went about his work. And so here the prophet is looking forward to a day when a sacred holiness would pervade all of life, even the most ordinary parts of it. The sermon was about the priesthood of all believers. I remember nothing of the detail of the message but I was struck by the text and by the topic and by the fact that it was such an interesting subject. It was something I had hardly ever heard of before then, and something I have rarely heard about since, except when delving into the subject myself.

For some reason, the priesthood of all believers is a subject on which one does not hear sermons—not in my evangelical circles, at least.

Introduction

It is the same when it comes to books. Apart from those by David Gay and Watchman Nee, from both of which I have learned without swallowing them whole, there is little at the popular level. More recently there has been a little booklet by Craig Troxel and books by Ed Welch (*Created to draw near*) and David Schrock (*The Royal Priesthood and the Glory of God*) which cover some of the material. At an academic level, there are Cyril Eastwood's *The Priesthood of All Believers: An Examination of the Doctrine from the Reformation to the Present Day* and *God's Mediators, a biblical theology of priesthood* by Andrew Malone, and maybe one or two other tomes, but not very much at all.

The need for a popular volume on this important subject would seem self-evident, therefore, and this little book seeks to provide it.

In his little booklet Dr Troxel helpfully warns against two extremes. The first error, he says, is to understate the priesthood of all believers by overstating the ministry of some. We can overstate the importance of pastors, elders and deacons. Yes, we must support, respect and pray for such people but they are not to be thought of as a different class of people and they must not think they are a cut above others.

The second error is to overstate the priesthood of all believers by understating the ordained ministry. Some argue that the priesthood of all believers does away with the need for an ordained ministry altogether. However, as Martin Luther (1483–1546) wrote, 'It is true that all Christians are priests, but not all are pastors.'

Unquestionably, Dr Troxel concludes, both the priesthood of all believers and the ministry of ordained officers are vital to the church's health and calling. The church's goal is not to maintain a balance between the two, but rather to encourage and engender the privileges and gifts of all members. The church needs every gift, every grace and every member, in order to grow properly.

Hopefully, this book neither overstates not understates the doctrine.

The book begins with an attempt to give some sort of biblical definition of priesthood and the characteristics of such priests and then seeks to identify who the actual priests are in our society today.

Then there is an important chapter on how to become a priest today.

Two chapters follow delineating what the differences are between priests in the Old Testament and priests in the New Testament and noting in what few ways they are similar.

There are then a couple of chapters, looking at several ways in which what is said in the rest of the book is important and needs to be taken note of.

The final chapter appropriately draws on a sermon by the Puritan Thomas Manton (1620–1677) considering the priesthood of the believer in heaven.

The Old Testament scholar Dr R. Laird Harris (1911–2008) once wrote:

First century Christianity had no priests. The New Testament nowhere uses the word to describe a leader in Christian service. The Jewish priesthood was changed, we are told in Hebrews 7:12. Christ is now our 'priest forever after the order of Melchizedek' (Hebrews 7:17). ... the Greek never uses the word 'hiereus' (priest), nor does the Latin so use 'sacerdos' (priest) ... Christian priests are a Roman Catholic invention.

When the New Testament talks about priesthood it is talking about the priesthood of ordinary believers. The sooner a Christian sees that, the better for him or for her.

12 The priesthood of all believers

1. Who are priests according to the Bible?

'And this all Christians ought to know: That the title of clergy St Peter gave to all God's people, till Pope Higinus and the succeeding prelates took it from them, appropriating that name to themselves and their priests only; and condemning the rest of God's inheritance to an injurious and alienate condition of laity ... imitating the old temple, and excluded the members of Christ' (John Milton).

'Appoint Aaron and his sons to serve as priests; anyone else who approaches the sanctuary is to be put to death.' The LORD also said to Moses, 'I have taken the Levites from among the Israelites in place of the first male offspring of every Israelite woman. The Levites are mine, for all the firstborn are mine. When I struck down all the firstborn in Egypt, I set apart for myself every firstborn in Israel, whether human or animal. They are to be mine. I am the LORD.'

Numbers 3:10–13

Picture a monk walking along with a hammer, some nails and a large piece of paper. Some sceptical historians have questioned the details but it is a famous scene from October 31, 1517. Martin Luther is about to nail his famous 95 theses to the door of the church of the castle of Wittenberg, Germany, unintentionally setting in motion the Reformation.

Luther was a man with great ideas and one of his ideas was the priesthood of all believers. The idea goes back at least as far as him and undoubtedly much further than that. Craig Troxel says that the church fathers—Justin Martyr, Tertullian, Irenaeus, Origin, Clement, Chrysostom, Cyprian and Augustine—all assumed it, and in the Middle Ages, Peter Lombard and Thomas Aquinas taught it as well. In the face of what had been going on in the church for over a thousand years, Luther hit back in his books *On the freedom of a Christian* and *Address to the German Nobility* with:

Whoever comes out of the water of baptism can boast that he is already a consecrated priest, bishop and pope, although of course it is not seemly that just anybody shall exercise such office.

And, referring, by way of example, to shoemakers and the block on which they make shoes:

Every shoemaker can be a priest of God, and stick to his own last while he does it.

The early church did speak of believers as a priestly race. However, by the middle of the third century after Christ's coming, things had changed. The idea that Christian ministers were mediatorial priests, promoted by the early church father Cyprian and others, became popular and that meant that increasingly other believers were demoted. The priesthood of all believers was pretty much lost sight of.

Medieval theologians taught that salvation comes through the church. It sounds innocent enough but the idea is that God works exclusively through a select class of priests who administer the so called seven sacraments of baptism, communion, confirmation, penance, extreme unction, marriage and holy orders.

In contrast Protestants teach the priesthood of all believers. The difference between the two views is that one view follows tradition and the other grows out of Scripture. As will be demonstrated, this doctrine is very much one taught in the Bible.

In order to consider the subject properly, it is useful to begin with two related questions.

First, who or what is a priest? If we want to have anything to do with religion, it is important to be able to answer that question with some certainty. This chapter will consider that question and then in Chapter 2 we will list a number of characteristics of a priest.

Later, in Chapter 3, we will come to a second question—who are true priests today? That is again a basic but important question that needs to be answered with some certainty.

There are plenty of people who claim the title *priest* today, or sometimes *priestess*, in the case of some women. Roman Catholics claim to have priests among them, as do Eastern Catholics and the Orthodox. Hindus, Buddhists, Shintoists, Taoists and Zoroastrians also claim the same. Mormons claim to have priests too, as do pagans or animists and practitioners of various occult religions. The Yoruba people of Nigeria have an ancient religion that has spread to other parts of the world. It involves a priesthood.

A BRIEF NOTE ON REFORMER MARTIN LUTHER

Martin Luther (1483–1546) was a German monk in the Augustan order who became a professor of theology and a central figure in the Protestant Reformation. Having become a Roman Catholic priest in 1507, his study of the Bible and the church fathers led him to deny several Romanist teachings and practices. It began with his rejection of the money making indulgence system and the production of his famous 95 theses of 1517. When challenged, he refused to retract his writings at the Diet of Worms before the Holy Roman Emperor Charles V in 1521. This led to Pope Leo X excommunicating him. Luther's central teaching was justification by faith through God's grace. Behind it lay his belief in the authority of the Bible, which he translated into German, acceptance of the sovereignty of God and the rejection of Papal authority. He also opposed sacerdotalism or priestcraft, considering all baptised Christians to be part of a holy priesthood.

Levites

Even a cursory examination of the Bible reveals that in the Old Testament period there were priests. For most of Israel's history these priests were all drawn from the same tribe in Israel and no other—the tribe of Levi. This is why people sometimes speak of:

- The Mosaic priesthood, because it began in the time of Moses.
- The Levitical priesthood, for though not all Levites were priests, all priests were Levites.
- The Aaronic priesthood, because Aaron, Moses' brother, was the first Levitical High Priest.

Before Israel is properly established you have non-Levites—Noah, Abraham, Melchizedek, Job—acting as priests. Indeed, God says to the people through Moses in Exodus 19:5–6:

Now if you obey me fully and keep my covenant, then out of all nations you will be my treasured possession. Although the whole earth is mine, you will be for me a kingdom of priests and a holy nation.

Because of the way it has sealed itself off from other nations North Korea is sometimes called *the hermit kingdom*. Some call mountainous Lesotho *the kingdom in the sky*. Thailand is known as *the land of smiles*, Chile as *the land of poets* and Iceland as *the land of ice and fire*. Ancient Israel was to be known as *a kingdom of priests*.

The original plan seems to have been that the head of each household, the eldest son from each family, would be priest to his own family. However, a new system was instituted in the time of Moses whereby the family of Aaron stood in for the firstborn in Israel and took on the responsibilities of priesthood with the assistance of their fellow members in the tribe of Levi.

The beginning of this arrangement is recorded in Exodus 32. It occurs after Moses has gone up Mount Sinai to receive the Ten Commandments. In the face of the idolatry with the golden calf that takes place while Moses is absent, first there is anger and then the Levites rally to Moses and take vengeance on their guilty brother Israelites, prompting Moses to say (32:29):

You have been set apart to the LORD today, for you were against your own sons and brothers, and he has blessed you this day.

And so, for example, in Numbers 3:10–13 God says that Aaron and his sons are to be appointed as priests and 'anyone else who approaches the sanctuary is to be put to death'. The LORD says to Moses that he has taken the Levites from among the Israelites 'in place of the first male offspring of every Israelite woman'. The logic is that all the firstborn in Israel are God's as when he struck down all the firstborn in Egypt he set them apart for himself, whether human or animal, and now the Levites belong to God in place of them. God says, 'They are to be mine. I am the LORD.'

A little later, in Numbers 3:41–48, we read about God saying to Moses that he is to count all the firstborn Israelite males a month old or more and list their names. The Levites were to be set aside to God in place of all the Israelite firstborn. Even the livestock of the Levites were to replace all the firstborn of the livestock of the other Israelites.

Because of the command, Moses lists all the firstborn males of the Israelites by name, finding that the total number a month old or more came at that time to 22,273. When the Levites are also counted there are found to be 273 less than firstborn Israelites. These 273 are then redeemed by collecting five shekels for each one. The money for redemption is given to Aaron and his sons.

So Moses is required to 'Take the Levites in place of all the firstborn of Israel, and the livestock of the Levites in place of their livestock.' The Levites are God's. He is the LORD.

Priesthood in the Old Testament then involved an anomaly. All the people belonged to God but not all of them were priests. Only Levites could be priests. These priests acted in a representative role, on behalf of the whole people. When Jeroboam rebelled against Rehoboam many years after Moses a mark of his apostate kingdom was the appointment of 'priests from all sorts of people, even though they were not Levites' (1 Kings 12:31; 13:33). The Samaritans later followed a similar policy (2 Kings 17:32).

The New Testament

When we come to the New Testament there is clearly a great change that takes place, a reversion we might say to something more like the original plan, a priesthood after the order of Melchizedek not of Aaron.

There are about 160 references to priests and priesthood in the New Testament. It is under the new covenant, as will be seen, that every true Christian believer becomes his or her own priest to God. Whatever other profession they may pursue—architect, baker, carpenter, doctor, electrician, farmer—they are also, each one, priests to God. Whether a gardener, a hairdresser, an illustrator, a judge, a knife grinder or a locksmith—every Christian is a priest to God. You may be a musician, a nurse, an optician, a preacher, a quarry worker, a radiographer or whatever—if you are a believer, you are also a priest.

This comes out in verses such as 1 Peter 2:5, where Peter tells believers that they themselves

like living stones, are being built into a spiritual house to be a holy priesthood, offering spiritual sacrifices acceptable to God through Jesus Christ.

In verse 9 of the same chapter, Peter says 'But you are a chosen people, a royal priesthood, a holy nation...'

This is how to understand Revelation 1:6. Revelation 5:10 says the same thing. God has made believers 'to be a kingdom and priests to serve our God'. That is how Revelation 20:6 should be taken, too:

Blessed and holy are those who share in the first resurrection [a reference to being born again]. The second death [hell] has no power over them, but they will be priests of God and of Christ and will reign with him for a thousand years [throughout the time between his first and second comings].

Old Testament prophecy

This is what is prophesied in the Old Testament. This is what lies behind the prophecy in Isaiah 61:6, for example:

And you will be called priests of the LORD, you will be named ministers of our God. You will feed on the wealth of nations, and in their riches you will boast.

Jamieson, Fausset and Brown comment that *And you* contrasts with the strangers spoken of in the previous verse, who do all the work. God's people are told that they shall have no need to attend to their flocks and lands but strangers will do it for them. Their exclusive business will be the service of Jehovah as his *priests*. Everything is put in Old Testament terms but it points to a New Testament reality.

Some wonderful verses in Zechariah 14:20–21 point in the same direction:

On that day HOLY TO THE LORD [the phrase that was inscribed on the gold plate that the High Priest wore] will be inscribed on the bells of the horses [the High Priest had bells on his sacred garment], and the cooking pots in the LORD's house will be like the sacred bowls in front of the altar. Every pot in Jerusalem and Judah will be holy to the LORD Almighty, and all who come to sacrifice will take some of the pots and cook in them.

Chapter 1

Malachi 1:11 is also relevant here:

'My name will be great among the nations, from where the sun rises to where it sets. In every place incense and pure offerings will be brought to me, because my name will be great among the nations,' says the LORD Almighty.

It is generally agreed among believers that the Old Testament is in some senses incomplete. Graeme Goldsworthy for example would say '...the Old Testament does not stand on its own, because it is incomplete without its conclusion and fulfilment in the person and work of Christ'. It anticipates something more in the future. One of the things it is looking forward to is the priesthood of all believers.

2. What are the characteristics of a priest according to the Bible?

'No man appoints himself to the priesthood but his appointment is of God. The priesthood is not a coveted office to be taken but a glorious privilege to which one is called. This latter point is applicable to all believers today, for all have been made priests in Christ Jesus' (Marcus Dods).

Every high priest is selected from among the people and is appointed to represent the people in matters related to God, to offer gifts and sacrifices for sins. He is able to deal gently with those who are ignorant and are going astray, since he himself is subject to weakness. This is why he has to offer sacrifices for his own sins, as well as for the sins of the people. And no one takes this honour on himself, but he receives it when called by God, just as Aaron was.

Hebrews 5:1–4

Contrasts are good for fixing ideas in our minds. I recall seeing a children's TV programme many years ago featuring a 'moth machine'. This wheeled contraption, when switched on by the presenter, would automatically travel toward the nearest source of light. At one point another presenter turned the vehicle's engine around and it became a 'mole machine' reversing away from the nearest source of light. The contrast helped illustrate the idea well.

We have really begun to answer our questions in part by way of introduction, but at this point we return to the original question afresh—*What is a priest, biblically speaking?* Further, *What are the characteristics of a priest, according to the Bible?* To answer these questions, first contrast prophets and priests.

Prophets and priests

Most people will have a general idea of who or what a priest is or what they do or are supposed to do. There are many false priests in this world, as well as true. A priest is supposed to be a mediator, a go-between, a bridge-builder, a conciliator; someone who is ideally able to bring a person to God.

It is useful in some ways to think of prophets and priests together.

- What is a prophet? He is a person who speaks to us on God's behalf. He is, as it were, God's means of coming to us.

This comes out at the beginning of Exodus 7 where the LORD says to Moses that he has made him 'like God to Pharaoh'. Moses was to speak all that God commanded him and his brother Aaron would also declare it to Pharaoh so that he would let the Israelites go. Moses' brother Aaron would be his prophet. He would speak on his behalf.

- What is a priest? He is a person who speaks to God on our behalf. He is, as it were, our means of coming to God.

Visualise a prophet as facing the people and speaking to them from God; visualise a priest as having his back to the people, leading them to God.

Hebrews 5:1–4

More specifically, on the subject of what priests are like, in Hebrews 5:1–4 we read that every high priest is to be selected from among the people and that he is appointed to represent them in matters related to God. This would include offering gifts and sacrifices for sins. Because he himself was a human being and so 'subject to weakness' he would be well able to deal gently with the people who by nature were ignorant and tended to go astray. Such a person would need first to offer sacrifices for his own sins and then also for the people's sins. The other thing there is that it is not something that one volunteers to do but a calling one receives when chosen by God, as in the case of Aaron, the first Levitical High Priest.

The writer to the Hebrews is concerned to define priesthood in connection with the priesthood of the Lord Jesus Christ, but what he says is of more general interest.

There are a number of things to notice:

- A priest serves human beings and so has to be a human being himself. It cannot very well be an angel or an animal for that matter or some sort of hybrid. It has to be one of the people. 'Every high priest is selected from among the people.'

- You cannot choose to be a true priest. You cannot volunteer. It is an appointment made by God. 'And no one takes this honour on himself,' says the writer to the Hebrews, 'but he receives it when called by God, just as Aaron was.'

- He is chosen to be the people's representative in anything to do with God. He 'is appointed to represent the people in matters related to God.'

- He offers gifts and sacrifices designed to remove sins. 'To offer gifts and sacrifices for sins.'

- From the Old Testament we learn that priests were involved in teaching the people about the law. In 2 Chronicles 17:9 we read of how in the reign of Jehoshaphat he sent out Levites who 'taught throughout Judah, taking with them the Book of the Law of the LORD; they went around to all the towns of Judah and taught the people'. This comes out in other places too, and here in Hebrews the writer talks about the priest being 'able to deal gently with those who are ignorant', suggesting an educative or teaching role.

- The Old Testament priests sought to turn the people to God, and here it speaks of the people not only being ignorant but also 'going astray'.

A BRIEF NOTE ON ROMANS 15:16

In Romans 15:16 Paul says of his ministry that God '... gave me the priestly duty of proclaiming the gospel of God, so that the Gentiles might become an offering acceptable to God, sanctified by the Holy Spirit'. This may seem to lend support to the idea that New Testament ministry is a form of priesthood, but Paul is merely using the idea of priesthood and sacrifices or offerings as a metaphor. In his ministry of proclaiming the gospel he has been like a priest making an offering of the Gentiles he sees converted, an offering acceptable to God. When converted they are sanctified by the Holy Spirit and so set apart as holy to God just as the sacrifices were set apart in ancient times. Paul does something similar in Philippians 2:17 when he speaks of himself as 'being poured out like a drink offering on the sacrifice and service coming from' the faith of the Philippians.

Other things that come out of an examination of the Old Testament priesthood that we ought also to note are these:

- The Old Testament priests had a duty to keep the Temple holy. This comes out in 2 Chronicles 23:6:

No one is to enter the temple of the LORD except the priests and Levites on duty; they may enter because they are consecrated, but all the others are to observe the LORD's command not to enter.

- It was also the privilege of the Levites and the priests to come regularly into the direct presence of God in the Temple. Think of how in 2 Chronicles 29:5, King Hezekiah says:

Listen to me, Levites! Consecrate yourselves now and consecrate the temple of the LORD, the God of your ancestors. Remove all defilement from the sanctuary.

- Further, it was the role of the Levites to lead the worship at the Temple, giving thanks to God (1 Chronicles 16) and to act as gatekeepers and guards at the Temple (1 Chronicles 26), keeping out unwanted elements (2 Chronicles 23:6).

- One final thing to mention is the way that in the Old Testament priests were instructed in how to bless the people. In Numbers 6:22–27 we read:

The LORD said to Moses, 'Tell Aaron and his sons, "This is how you are to bless the Israelites. Say to them: 'The LORD bless you and keep you; the LORD make his face shine on you and be gracious to you; the LORD turn his face toward you and give you peace.'" So they will put my name on the Israelites, and I will bless them.'

To sum up the chief characteristics of a priest then:

- First, *qualifications:* being a human being and being appointed by God.

- Second, *the role:* being in a representative capacity.

- Third, *what is involved:* giving gifts and making sacrifices; teaching people the law and turning them to God; maintaining holiness and being in the presence of God; worshipping and giving thanks; guarding the way to God; blessing the people.

A person who knows what a priest is will be more likely to know who is one when they see one, and who is not one when a false claim is made.

Having given a good idea of what a priest is, one is better placed to answer the next question: *Who are true priests today?*

3. Who are true priests today?

'As early as 1520, Luther had laid the fundamental conceptual foundations for created sacred space within the secular. His doctrine of the 'priesthood of all believers' asserted that there is no genuine difference of status between the 'spiritual' and the 'temporal' order. All Christians are called to be priests—and can exercise that calling within the everyday world. The idea of 'calling' was fundamentally redefined: no longer … about being called to serve God by leaving the world; it was now about serving God in the world' (Alister E. McGrath).

As you come to him, the living Stone—rejected by humans but chosen by God and precious to him—you also, like living stones, are being built into a spiritual house to be a holy priesthood, offering spiritual sacrifices acceptable to God through Jesus Christ.

1 Peter 2:4–5

The late Franco Maggiotto was an Italian with a remarkable story. He often recalled the day when one Sunday morning, as a Roman Catholic priest, he was leading a sung Mass with two other priests, a throng of young people in white either side of him and a choir singing beautiful music. At the foot of the altar, Franco was praying, asking God to destroy him, he was in such confusion and agony. While he washed his hands at the altar, a young man was reading Hebrews 10:10. It was a shock to Franco's mind. While he was battling in his heart, he heard, 'By the which will we are sanctified through the offering of the body of Jesus Christ once for all.' He spoke to himself, telling himself off for his stupidity, for not seeing what Jesus Christ has done. It was like a hammer in his mind, 'and every priest standeth daily ministering and offering often times the same sacrifices which can never take away sins'. Franco spoke to the priests with him, 'Do you hear him? Have you heard him?' They looked at each other. 'Look, look what is written here,' he continued, 'He did the job, we are useless. He has done the job and their sins I will remember no more. He did the job, we are useless.' Franco was so happy he cried and laughed. He had finally understood that the sort of priest that he had been trying to be is really redundant. He was about to become another sort of priest altogether.

Once it is clear as to what a priest is, then the second question can be addressed—who are true priests today? As has been noted, there are many people who claim to be priests today, as Franco Maggiotto once did before his conversion, but are they really priests in truth?

The Roman Catholic idea

The official Roman Catholic Catechism asks the question *What is the role of the priest?* The answer given is that

A priest first of all is a baptised man who has heard God calling him to a particular role in the Church—that of ministerial priesthood. After usually about six or seven years training he is ordained.

As to who is a priest? The answer given is this:

The priest is first and foremost a man of prayer. The priest lives in *persona Christi*, so his most important prayer is to re-present the sacrifice of Jesus during Holy Mass. His parish relies on him to offer a sacrifice 'holy and acceptable to God'.

So, according to Roman teaching, a priest has to be male, has to be baptised, has to be called to a particular role by God and needs six or seven years training before he can start. He is a man of prayer, who represents Christ and whose most important role is connected with the Roman Catholic Mass, which claims to be a re-sacrificing of the body of Christ. His parish relies on him to do this—it is something they cannot do for themselves.

A BRIEF NOTE ON THE WORD PRIEST

It is perhaps worth mentioning that in English there is a linguistic issue concerning the word *priest*. Perhaps you have heard that quotation from John Milton: 'New Presbyter is but old priest writ large.' At the time he was complaining that Protestantism had not brought as many changes as it was supposed to have done. However, the idea that the words *priest* and *presbyter* or *elder* are connected is undoubtedly true. Our word *priest* is most likely to have come, through Latin, from the Greek word for *elder (presbuteros)* rather than from one meaning priest. English ended up then with the same term (priest) for the presbyter or elder, who presides over and instructs a Christian congregation, and a priest, one who offers sacrifices, especially once the communion came to be seen as an unbloody sacrifice. You can see then why some Anglican ministers who are thoroughly biblical in so many respects are still quite happy to be called *priests*.

Now the New Testament does talk about baptism and about prayer, but in every other way this idea of priesthood is very different indeed from the New Testament one. At best, in fact, it is only a reversion to the Old Testament system.

New Testament priests should indeed be baptised and prayerful but they can be male or female; they can be called to any number of different roles and they do not always need special training of a formal sort before carrying out their tasks. Rather than seeking to make a fresh sacrifice of Christ, they rely on the sacrifice that their High Priest has already made for them once for all and that delivers them from their sins.

It is true that there are certain men who are called exclusively to preach God's Word, but the distinction that Roman Catholicism tries to make between a priesthood and a laity is a human invention, not the pattern laid down in the New Testament. No, all men and women who have been truly converted are priests to God under the one great High Priest, Jesus Christ. It is God who sets them aside, who consecrates them to himself.

Writing on the Christian ministry in the late 19th century Bishop J. B. Lightfoot (1828–1889) observes correctly that:

The kingdom of Christ, not being a kingdom of the world, is not limited by the restrictions which fetter other societies, political or religious. It has no sacred days or seasons, no special sanctuaries, because every time and place alike are holy. Above all, it has no sacerdotal [i.e. priestly] system. It interposes no sacrificial tribe or class between God and man, by whose intervention alone God is reconciled, and man forgiven.

The biblical idea

The fact is that the moment a person turns from their sins and puts his or her faith in Jesus Christ, that person is a Christian. Now whether that person goes on to be a minister or preacher or not, that person is already a priest in the biblical sense.

Professor J. V. Fesko has defined the priesthood of all believers like this:

The doctrine of the priesthood of all believers states that all believers in Christ share in his priestly status; therefore, there is no special class of people who mediate the knowledge, presence, and forgiveness of Christ to the rest of believers, and all believers have the right and authority to read, interpret, and apply the teachings of Scripture.

That means several things for you, then, if you are a Christian today. If you are a believer:

• Through Jesus Christ, you are able to go to God on your own behalf and also on behalf of others.

• You are able to make sacrifices to God. 1 Peter 2:5 includes a reference to 'offering spiritual sacrifices acceptable to God through Jesus Christ'.

What are these spiritual sacrifices? The New Testament specifies in various places:

Faith (Philippians 2:17): 'But even if I am being poured out like a drink offering on the sacrifice and service coming from your faith, I am glad and rejoice with all of you.'

Praise (Hebrews 13:15): 'Through Jesus, therefore, let us continually offer to God a sacrifice of praise—the fruit of lips that openly profess his name.'

Prayer (Revelation 5:8): 'And when he had taken it, the four living creatures and the twenty-four elders fell down before the Lamb. Each one had a harp and they were holding golden bowls full of incense, which are the prayers of God's people.'

Sharing with others (Hebrews 13:16): 'And do not forget to do good and to share with others, for with such sacrifices God is pleased. In Philippians 4:18 Paul says of the gifts the Philippians sent him: 'They are a fragrant offering, an acceptable sacrifice, pleasing to God.'

All of life (Romans 12:1): 'Therefore, I urge you, brothers and sisters, in view of God's mercy, to offer your bodies as a living sacrifice, holy and pleasing to God—this is your true and proper worship.'

• You are able to teach people the law and, by God's grace, turn them to God. You have the authority to read the Bible for yourself and interpret and apply it to yourself and to others. There is an overlap here between the Christian being a priest and being a prophet. In Colossians 3:16 Paul urges believers to let the message of Christ dwell among them richly as they teach and admonish one another with all wisdom singing to God, 'psalms, hymns, and songs from the Spirit' with gratitude in their hearts.

In Romans 15:14 he says he is convinced that his brothers and sisters are all themselves full of goodness, filled with knowledge and competent to instruct one another.

Then in Jude 22–23 we read that believers are to be merciful to those who doubt, to save others by snatching them from the fire and by showing mercy, mixed with fear; to yet others, 'hating even the clothing stained by corrupted flesh'.

Finally, in 1 Peter 3:15–16 it says that believers are to revere Christ in their hearts as Lord, always being prepared to give an answer to everyone who asks them to give the reason for the hope that they have. This is to be done 'with gentleness and respect, keeping a clear conscience'. The aim is to make 'those who speak maliciously against your good behaviour in Christ' ashamed of their slander.

- You can maintain holiness and come into the presence of God. There are many calls to holiness in the New Testament. In 1 Thessalonians 4:7 Paul says, 'God did not call us to be impure, but to live a holy life.' Then in Hebrews 10:19–22 there are those wonderful words:

Therefore, brothers and sisters, since we have confidence to enter the Most Holy Place by the blood of Jesus, by a new and living way opened for us through the curtain, that is, his body, and since we have a great priest over the house of God …

There is no room to say more about this here but it goes on to urge believers to draw near to God 'with a sincere heart and with the full assurance that faith brings' their hearts sprinkled to cleanse them from a guilty conscience and 'their bodies washed with pure water'.

- It is your duty and privilege to worship God and to serve him.

- It is also your duty to guard the way to God. You yourself are separated to God and must be holy and you are to encourage holiness in others.

- It is your privilege to be a blessing to other believers. As a priest, it is your calling not merely to pronounce words of blessing on others but to be a real means under God of bringing spiritual peace and happiness to his people. By means of our prayers, our words, our acts of kindness, we can bless others, even those who are older or more mature in the faith than we.

***

If you are reading this and you are a Christian; if you are trusting in the Lord Jesus Christ, then you are a priest of God Most High. What glorious privileges are yours—and what great responsibilities too. Be thankful to God and seek to serve him always.

Martin Luther, whom we have quoted already, said rightly:

All Christians are altogether priests, and let it be anathema to assert there is any other priest than he who is Christian; for it will be asserted without the Word of God, on no authority but the sayings of men, or the antiquity of custom, or the multitude of those that think so.

This is what the Word of God truly teaches. If only it were better known!

4. How do you become a true priest today?

'The priest is not made. He must be born a priest; must inherit his office. I refer to the new birth—the birth of water and the Spirit. Thus all Christians must become priests, children of God and co-heirs with Christ the Most High Priest' (Martin Luther).

But you have an anointing from the Holy One, and all of you know the truth. ... As for you, the anointing you received from him remains in you, and you do not need anyone to teach you. But as his anointing teaches you about all things and as that anointing is real, not counterfeit—just as it has taught you, remain in him.

1 John 2:20, 27

When you first read Psalm 133 it is rather strange. It uses two unusual pictures to describe Christian unity. The first is that of precious oil being poured on the head and running down on the beard and on the collar of someone's robe. The head and beard and robe in mind are those of Aaron the first Levitical High Priest. It is the day he is anointed as High Priest. Aaron no doubt never forgot the day he became a High Priest.

So far we have looked at two main questions: 'Who or what is a priest?' and 'Who are true priests today?' We observed that there are plenty of people today claiming the title *priest* or sometimes *priestess* in the case of women. Roman Catholics, Hindus, Buddhists and Pagans all claim to have priests among them. It is clear too that in the Old Testament certain of God's people were priests, eventually certain people exclusively from the tribe of Levi.

To the first question, in Chapter 1, it has been said, firstly, that to be a priest you must be a human being and you must be appointed by God. Then the point was made that it involves being in a representative capacity (representing a person to God—it could be yourself or it could be someone else). Thirdly, there was what is involved—giving gifts and making sacrifices, teaching people the law and turning them to God, maintaining holiness and being in the presence of God, worship and guarding what is holy, blessing people.

In Chapter 2, the question was, who are true priests today? Although many claim to be priests, the truth is that the only real priests are Christian believers, male and female. Such people, and such people alone, can go to God through Christ on their own behalf and also on behalf of others. They also are able to make acceptable sacrifices to God and teach people the law and, by God's grace, turn them to God. Only they can maintain holiness and come into the immediate presence of God and only they truly worship God and guard what is holy and bless his people.

Next come two further related questions that will help to open up the subject of the priesthood of all believers a little further. In this chapter the subject is how a person becomes a New Testament priest. It has already been stated that to be a priest you must do certain things, but here the subject, more narrowly, is how you become a priest. It does not involve pouring oil on a person's head.

In the next two chapters, in order to sharpen our understanding further, the differences between Old Testament Levites and priests and New Testament priests will be explored.

The answer to the first question is to be found in Revelation 1:5–6. There we read of

Jesus Christ, who is the faithful witness, the firstborn from the dead, and the ruler of the kings of the earth.

It then says:

To him who loves us and has freed us from our sins by his blood, and has made us to be a kingdom and priests to serve his God and Father—to him be glory and power for ever and ever! Amen.

Do note that it is Jesus Christ, according to these believers, who has loved us

and has freed us from our sins by his blood, and has made us to be a kingdom and priests to serve his God and Father.

To be a priest you need to be a human being and you need to be appointed by God. It is those who are appointed to priesthood by Jesus Christ who are truly priests.

You can see the same thing elsewhere. In Revelation 5 they praise the Lamb and say in verse 10 'You [the Lamb] have made them [believers] to be a kingdom and priests to serve our God, and they will reign on the earth.'

In 1 Peter 2:5, Peter says to believers:

you also, like living stones, are being built into a spiritual house to be a holy priesthood.

Before that (2:2–3) he says:

Like newborn babies, crave pure spiritual milk, so that by it you may grow up in your salvation, now that you have tasted that the Lord is good.

The priesthood here is to be like newborn babies, craving spiritual milk. The reference to new born babies takes us back to verse 23 of the previous chapter where Peter says:

For you have been born again, not of perishable seed, but of imperishable, through the living and enduring word of God.

It is by being born again that you become a priest to God. At the very beginning of Peter's first letter he says of God (1:3):

In his great mercy he has given us new birth into a living hope through the resurrection of Jesus Christ from the dead.

Jesus says in John 3:5:

Very truly I tell you, no one can enter the kingdom of God unless they are born of water and the Spirit.

There needs to be washing and renewal then. Titus 3:4 and 5 is similar. Paul says there:

But when the kindness and love of God our Saviour appeared, he saved us, not because of righteous things we had done, but because of his mercy. He saved us through the washing of rebirth and renewal by the Holy Spirit.

It is interesting in this respect that in Numbers 8:5–7 we read how Moses is commanded to take the Levites from among all the Israelites 'and make them ceremonially clean'. In order to purify them he is first to 'sprinkle the water of cleansing on them' and then to 'have them shave their whole bodies and wash their clothes'. By this means they were to be purified.

So their purification involved a washing and a shaving, symbolic of becoming like little babies again. There were also sacrifices and other rituals required. They point forward to what needs to happen for a person to become a true priest today.

So in Leviticus 8 we read how Aaron and his sons were ordained by means of sacrifices, being dressed in priestly garments, being anointed with oil and being marked with blood.

Such details remind us of at least four things:

First, that the sacrifice of Christ on the cross is the ground for the believer's priesthood. Christ 'gave himself for us to redeem us from all lawlessness and to purify for himself a people for his own possession who are zealous for good works' (Titus 2:14).

Second, that we can serve as priests only because he has provided garments of righteousness for us that cover our sins. This comes out in a verse like Zechariah 3:4:

The angel said to those who were standing before him, 'Take off his filthy clothes.' Then he said to Joshua, 'See, I have taken away your sin, and I will put fine garments on you.'

A BRIEF NOTE ON EXODUS 29:20

To an Old Testament Israelite, the different parts of the body were symbolic of different aspects of life. How would they have understood what is described in this verse?

- The ear lobe stands for the ear: hearing the word of God.
- The thumb stands for the hand: doing the work of God.
- The toe stands for the foot: walking in the way of God.

The ceremony was teaching them that to be priests in God's house they had to be careful to listen to God, use their hands in his service and walk in his ways. Presumably, it was too messy to smear blood on the whole ear, the whole hand or the whole foot. So a small part was chosen to make the point. Being a priest was a whole lifestyle, it was not just a 9 to 5 job. Whenever they used their ears, their hands or their feet, they were to use them for God. So must we who are their successors today.

Third, that believers have an anointing—not merely of oil, symbolic of the Spirit, but of the Holy Spirit himself. The Spirit within sets apart to the priesthood. See 1 John 2:20, 27:

But you have an anointing from the Holy One, and all of you know the truth. ... As for you, the anointing you received from him remains in you, and you do not need anyone to teach you. But as his anointing teaches you about all things and as that anointing is real, not counterfeit—just as it has taught you, remain in him.

Fourth, just as when the Old Testament priests were presented to God and Moses was told to

... take some ... blood and put it on the lobes of the right ears of Aaron and his sons, on the thumbs of their right hands, and on the big toes of their right feet

so we must listen to God's instructions, do what he says and go where he sends.

Be clear then on how to become a priest. Roman Catholics say you need to be trained for six or seven years. To be a Zen Buddhist priest involves a minimum one year of preparation and then a five year commitment to continuous training before you can even be considered.

In contrast, what needs to happen in order to become a true priest is that you need to be born again—regenerated. That is the vital thing. Are you born again? If you are, then you are a priest to God in the New Testament sense. There is no other way in.

5. What are the differences between Old and New Covenant priests?

'The primary purpose of an Old Testament priest was to offer acceptable sacrifices to God on behalf of the people. Priests were chosen by God ... specially cleansed through prescribed ceremonies, clothed in a prescribed manner ... anointed with oil ... Those qualifications are paralleled in Christians, whom God regards as the only true priests. ... The priesthood of believers is a high and holy calling to which no one is suited apart from God's grace and power' (John MacArthur).

Now if the ministry that brought death, which was engraved in letters on stone, came with glory, so that the Israelites could not look steadily at the face of Moses because of its glory, transitory though it was, will not the ministry of the Spirit be even more glorious?

2 Corinthians 3:7–8

At the beginning of his prophecy, the prophet Ezekiel tells us that it was the thirtieth year. An obvious question is, the thirtieth year since when? The consensus among the commentators seems to be that it was thirty years since Ezekiel was born. The significance of this is that Ezekiel was a Levitical priest and at the very moment when he would have been starting his priestly work, he found himself over 700 miles away from the Temple in exile in Babylon. One can only begin to imagine the disappointed yearning of a man who had no doubt dreamed of this moment from his youngest days and yet who now knew it would never happen. It is not an experience a New Testament priest will ever have to face.

A useful thing to do in order to explore the subject further is to think of the differences and similarities between the Old Testament Levites and priests and New Testament priests, that is, believers today. At least six differences can be noted. We will look at several of the differences in this chapter and at more differences and at the similarities in the next chapter.

They are under different covenants

The first and most obvious thing is that the two serve under different covenants. The first covenant, the old covenant, was temporary while the new covenant is eternal. The old covenant was very much to do with the outward rather than the inward. The new covenant is much more to do with the inward rather than the outward. The old covenant was highly symbolic; the new covenant is real. Most importantly, the old covenant was a covenant that brought death while the new covenant brings life. Paul speaks in 2 Corinthians 3:6 of being a minister 'of a new covenant—not of the letter but of the Spirit; for the letter kills, but the Spirit gives life'. He adds:

Now if the ministry that brought death, which was engraved in letters on stone, came with glory, so that the Israelites could not look steadily at the face of Moses because of its glory, transitory though it was, will not the ministry of the Spirit be even more glorious?

The Levites served under a glorious covenant. The shining of Moses' face highlights that fact. But those who serve as New Testament priests serve under a covenant that is even more glorious.

Yes, there was something glorious about the Temple with all its rich furnishings and the priests in their glorious robes. The ritual involved hundreds and hundreds of animals being sacrificed and all sorts of ceremonies and laws. The new covenant is ever so much more subtle and spiritual. Outwardly, it sometimes seems to have little going for it, perhaps, but that is not the case at all.

For example, the sacrifices of the Old Testament priests could never take away sin. No one sacrifice nor all of them put together could do such a thing. That is why they carried on being made.

Those priests kept dying, of course, including the High Priest. Now when a High Priest died it was a time for releasing people from their debts and from other stipulations, but the priests kept dying without actually bringing in a solution. Under the new covenant the High Priest is Jesus Christ, and though he was crucified he rose again and now he ever lives to intercede for his own. He never dies. His one sacrifice—the sacrifice of himself—has taken away the sins of all his people and he is now High Priest over a royal priesthood, who, though they die, have eternal life in him.

In Hebrews 9:9–15 we are told that the Old Testament worship is only about 'food and drink and various ceremonial washings—external regulations applying until the time of the new order'. With the coming of Christ 'as high priest of the good things that are now already here', unlike the Aaronic High Priest, he did not go through a tabernacle made with human hands but 'the greater and more perfect tabernacle that is not made with human hands, that is to say, is not a part of this creation'. Further, he did not enter 'by means of the blood of goats and calves' but he did it once for all 'by his own blood, thus obtaining eternal redemption'.

As the writer notes, 'the blood of goats and bulls and the ashes of a heifer sprinkled on those who are ceremonially unclean sanctify them so that they are outwardly clean' how much more, then, will Christ's blood, offered 'through the eternal Spirit', an unblemished sacrifice, cleanse the consciences of believers 'from acts that lead to death, so that they may serve the living God!' This is the reason why 'Christ is the mediator of a new covenant, that those who are called may receive the promised eternal inheritance'. That is the situation now that Christ has 'died as a ransom' to set his people 'free from the sins committed under the first covenant'.

One priesthood makes physical, the other spiritual, sacrifices

It is worth underlining the fact that whereas in the Old Testament physical sacrifices of animals and of food and drink were made, under the new covenant it is spiritual sacrifices that are made. We have previously quoted 1 Peter 2:5:

you also, like living stones, are being built into a spiritual house to be a holy priesthood, offering spiritual sacrifices acceptable to God through Jesus Christ.

Even in the Old Testament there is an awareness that it is the spiritual sacrifices that God ultimately wants. See, for example:

Psalm 50:14,23: 'Sacrifice thank offerings to God, fulfil your vows to the Most High, ... Those who sacrifice thank offerings honour me, and to the blameless I will show my salvation.'

Psalm 51:15–17: 'Open my lips, Lord, and my mouth will declare your praise. You do not delight in sacrifice, or I would bring it; you do not take pleasure in burnt offerings. My sacrifice, O God, is a broken spirit; a broken and contrite heart you, God, will not despise.'

Psalm 141:1–2: 'I call to you, LORD, come quickly to me; hear me when I call to you. May my prayer be set before you like incense; may the lifting up of my hands be like the evening sacrifice.'

A BRIEF NOTE ON BLESSING THE CONGREGATION

It is a tradition in many churches to close the worship service with a benediction, usually drawn from the New Testament letters or the Aaronic blessing in Numbers. Sometimes when a new minister is ordained he will be asked to pronounce the benediction at the end of the service. Sometimes objections are raised to such a practice because it gives the impression that the minister is a priest. Some seek to circumvent the problem by having the congregation pronounce a blessing on themselves together: 'May the grace of the Lord Jesus Christ ... be with us all'. The concern is legitimate but the remedy is not necessary. Given that a minister or anyone else leading the service for that matter is a true Christian then he is a priest and there can be no objection to him formally blessing the congregation, saying 'May the grace of the Lord Jesus Christ ... be with you all.' He may even raise his hands as he does so.

One priesthood was for special times and special places, the other for all times and all places

The Old Testament priests served chiefly in the Temple in Jerusalem. There were other duties but the chief thing was the Temple. At the Temple there were rotas so that everyone knew when he was serving and in what particular capacity. You can read all about it in 1 Chronicles 23–26. There were sacrifices at a certain time every morning and every evening and every week and every month and every year. Under the new covenant a priest is always on duty. He does not have to be in church to serve but serves, rather, wherever he finds himself.

In one case, what matters is birth; in the other, new birth

We have already made the point that to become a new covenant priest you need to be born again. So whereas under the old covenant it was a matter of birth—if you were a son of Levi, of a certain age and nothing else prohibited it, you took up priestly duties—under the new covenant it is a matter of new birth. In one sense, who your parents or family are makes no difference. What really matters is that you are born again, born from above by the power of the Spirit.

In one case, a few serve the Lord but in the other it is all

Another obvious difference is that whereas in Old Testament Israel it was only the Levites who served as priests, under the new covenant it is every member of that covenant community that serves as a priest. In Numbers 8:24–25 we read that the regulations about serving apply to Levite men from the age of twenty-five years old and up. They are to 'take part in the work at the tent of meeting'. At the age of fifty 'they must retire from their regular service and work no longer'.

Under the old covenant only males could serve; under the new covenant, it is males and females. Under the old covenant not all Levites served as priests, only certain ones. Again, under the new covenant, it is all. All are to take up its duties, all know its privileges. There were also age restrictions under the old covenant. You had to be a certain age to serve: between 25 and 50. All this has also gone in Christ. New Testament priests serve from the day they are born again until the day they die and pass on to their heavenly reward. They may officially retire from their day job but they continue to serve as priests, nevertheless.

6. What further differences are there between Old and New Covenant priests and what are some similarities?

'As the church displays ... spiritual graces, her attraction surpasses the ornate beauty of Aaron's robe. The beauty she exhibits as a nation of priests is that of her High Priest. And the exercise of her apportioned gifts ascends before God as fragrant offerings, pleasing and acceptable to him, because they are offered not just in Christ's name but also for his honour (Philippians 4:18)' (Craig Troxel).

In this way you are to set the Levites apart from the other Israelites, and the Levites will be mine.

Numbers 8:14

The name of George Stott is not well known in the annals of missionary endeavour. His story deserves to be better known. Stott, a Scotsman, was one of the first recruits to the China Inland Mission founded by J. Hudson Taylor (1832–1905) in 1865. He came to faith at the age of 21 while recuperating from an operation to remove his leg. After working for several years as a teacher, he heard about the needs of China and determined to go. He became the first Protestant missionary to work in Wenzhou, a city that now traces its large, vibrant church to this one-legged saint. When asked how he could do this on one leg, he replied, 'I do not see those with two legs going, so I must.' Stott is typical of a new priesthood where something like the lack of a leg is no barrier to usefulness in the kingdom.

Having looked at several differences between Old Testament and New Testament priests in the previous chapter, this chapter considers some more differences and then two similarities.

In one case physical perfection is required, in the other perfection in Christ

Another thing about Old Testament priests is that they had to meet certain physical requirements of perfection. In Leviticus 21:17–24 we read how Moses is told to tell Aaron that 'For the generations to come' none of his descendants can 'come near to offer the food of his God who has a defect'. No man who has any defect may come near. This would include anyone who was affected in the following ways due to an injury or a birth defect. If he was:

- blind
- lame
- facially disfigured
- deformed in any part of his body
- suffering foot problems due to club foot or something similar
- suffering hand problems due to Dupuytren's contracture or some other issue
- suffering from kyphosis making him a hunchback
- of restricted growth as in dwarfism
- plagued by an eye defect such as myopia, hyperopia, perhaps even a squint, a lazy eye or colour blindness

- suffering dermatological problems such as festering or running sores
- found to have damaged testicles.

No descendant of Aaron the priest who had any defect was to present food offerings to God. Such people were allowed to eat 'the most holy food' of their God and the holy food other Levites ate, but because of his defect he could not enter the Temple. That would be to desecrate God's sanctuary.

Under the new covenant no such rules apply. Being blind or short sighted or disfigured or deformed is not a problem as far as serving God as a New Testament priest is concerned. People with curvature of the spine or diminished stature or confined to a wheel chair, those with running sores or other diseases—all are welcome. All that matters is that you are born again and justified by faith. There have been outstanding examples of people who, despite their disabilities, have faithfully served the Lord. Christmas Evans (1766-1838) the one-eyed preacher, Fanny Crosby (1820–1915) the blind hymn writer and Joni Eareckson Tada the paraplegic author, artist and radio host are well known examples. Lesser known examples include John Kitto, the nineteenth century Bible scholar, deaf from the age of twelve; J. Charles Beckwith, the general with a wooden leg, who after being maimed at Waterloo devoted his time and money to helping the Waldensian church in Northern Italy; and Bethany Hamilton the American professional surfer whose left arm was bitten off by a shark in 2003 and whose story is told in the book and film *Soul Surfer*.

A BRIEF NOTE ON JOHN KITTO

Plymouth born John Kitto (1804–1854) was a sickly child. His father's drunkenness and his family's poverty meant that much of his childhood was spent in the workhouse. When he was twelve he fell from a rooftop and became totally and permanently deaf. Further tragedies and disappointments followed and there was much loneliness. He was only 4 ft 8 in and his accident left him with impaired balance. Although poorly educated, he became an eager reader and began to pen newspaper articles. He found a job in a local library where he continued to educate himself but later gained employment in the dental practice of Brethren pioneer Anthony Norris Groves, in Exeter. In 1829 he travelled to the Middle East with the Groves family and later wrote about his experiences back in England, where he married and had several children. He went on to produce several books mainly on Bible subjects, some of which continue to be in print today.

Only under the New Covenant can priests be royal priests

One of the characteristics of the Old Testament law was that it would not allow kings to be priests. You may have read how King Uzzah went into the Temple to offer incense and was struck with leprosy as a punishment (see 2 Chronicles 26).

In contrast, Martin Luther in his *Treatise of Christian Liberty* wrote:

Who then can comprehend the lofty dignity of the Christian? By virtue of his royal power he rules over all things, death, life, and sin, and through his priestly glory is omnipotent with God because he does the things which God asks and desires, as it is written, *He will fulfil the desire of those who fear him; he also will hear their cry and save them* [cf. Phil. 4:13]. To this glory a man attains, certainly not by any works of his, but by faith alone.

The Christian has both a kingly and a priestly calling. The kingly is much more in the future but even now we are more than conquerors and all things are ours. God's grace is sufficient and we sit in the heavenly places with Christ. We are *priests of God and of Christ and we reign with him* throughout this millennial period.

In one case entrance to God is restricted, in the other unrestricted

Under the Old Testament Law there were many rules and regulations. One was that only the High Priest could go into the Holiest Place of all and that only once a year and then carrying the blood of a goat. When Jesus died on the cross the curtain before the Holiest Place was torn in two from top to bottom, symbolising the opening up of a new and living way into God's presence for all who put their faith in Christ. We are now free to pray to God from any place and at any time. We can simply go into his immediate presence wherever we are. We must be reverent, of course, but we are free to go in. What a glorious privilege!

In the letter to the Hebrews the writer says, first, in Hebrews 4:14–16:

Therefore, since we have a great high priest who has ascended into heaven, Jesus the Son of God, let us hold firmly to the faith we profess. For we do not have a high priest who is unable to empathise with our weaknesses, but we have one who has been tempted in every way, just as we are—yet he did not sin. Let us then approach God's throne of grace with confidence, so that we may receive mercy and find grace to help us in our time of need.

Then later, in Hebrews 10:19–22, he says that 'since we have confidence to enter the Most Holy Place by the blood of Jesus, by a new and living way opened for us through … his body, and since we have a great priest over the house of God' we ought to draw near to God with sincere hearts, fully assured in our faith and 'having our hearts sprinkled to cleanse us from a guilty conscience'.

Finally, there are two similarities worth noting.

In both cases there is a setting apart to God

In Numbers 8:14 God instructs Moses:

In this way you are to set the Levites apart from the other Israelites, and the Levites will be mine.

Back in Numbers 3 the Levites had been singled out. It bears comparison with the way God has separated the church to himself, that is priests of the New Testament. In John 17:9 we read the words of Jesus:

I pray for them. I am not praying for the world, but for those you have given me, for they are yours.

Ephesians 2:13 says:

But now in Christ Jesus you who once were far away have been brought near by the blood of Christ.

In both cases priests teach, intercede, bless people and praise God, though in different ways

As we have suggested, the Old Testament priests taught the people, prayed for them, led them in giving praise to God and blessed them. There is a sense in which New Testament priests do the same things although there are clear differences.

We know that Levites taught the Law. In Leviticus 10:11 they are told:

And so you can teach the Israelites all the decrees the LORD has given them through Moses.

We read about it in the books of Chronicles too. Under the new covenant (Colossians 3:16) Christians are to

Let the message of Christ dwell among you richly as you teach and admonish one another with all wisdom through psalms, hymns, and songs from the Spirit, singing to God with gratitude in your hearts.

Like Samuel and Ezra, the priests prayed for the people, they made intercession for them. Again we ought to pray for ourselves and for others. There are many exhortations to pray in the New Testament. Praising God in the Temple was a big part of their work, especially from the time of David. We too must engage in that work.

New Testament worship is very different from Temple worship but worship must go on. Jesus says (John 4:23–24):

a time is coming and has now come when the true worshippers will worship the Father in the Spirit and in truth, for they are the kind of worshippers the Father seeks. God is spirit, and his worshippers must worship in the Spirit and in truth.

Then the priests blessed the people. They are told how to bless people at the end of Numbers 6. We still use the formula today. We too should bless people not only in word but also in deed.

7. What are the reasons why the priesthood of all believers matters?

'... ordinary people now have the Spirit of God and do the work of ministry. Everyone is busy and needed. Our mission is to be close to the Lord, invite others to come closer to him, and speak words of blessing in the name of Jesus' (Edward T. Welch).

Every high priest is selected from among the people and is appointed to represent the people in matters related to God, to offer gifts and sacrifices for sins. He is able to deal gently with those who are ignorant and are going astray, since he himself is subject to weakness. This is why he has to offer sacrifices for his own sins, as well as for the sins of the people. And no one takes this honour on himself, but he receives it when called by God, just as Aaron was.

Hebrews 5:1–4

'What's the point?' This is the age old question that generations of school children have asked of their teachers, especially those dealing with mathematics, science, French and sundry other subjects. The question is especially popular on warm Friday afternoons. Geoffrey Willans' character Nigel Molesworth asked the question of his sadistic maths master Arbuthnot and was not satisfied when he tried to explain that mathematics is a sort of language well worth learning. I did once hear the rock guitarist Francis Rossi admit that his French teacher had been right to argue, as she had, that by learning French Rossi would have been able to use it when he eventually went on tour to France to play guitar, his childhood ambition.

The subject is the priesthood of all believers, the fact that in this New Testament period, between Christ's first and second comings, every Christian believer is a priest to God under the one great High Priest, Jesus Christ. Already we have taken note of several Scriptures that point in this direction.

At this point it is good to consider why all this matters. We want to say a number of things in this chapter and some more in the next.

It is a biblical principle

If it is in the Bible then it must be significant to some extent. Now it is true that it is not obviously a prominent doctrine on the face of it, but it certainly is there and that means that it must be important for us to know these things.

We have noted verses such as 1 Peter 2:5 where Peter tells believers that, like living stones, they are being built into a spiritual house to be a holy priesthood. As priests they offer spiritual sacrifices that are acceptable to God through Jesus Christ.

In verse 9, he says to believers that they 'are a chosen people, a royal priesthood, a holy nation...'

As stated, this is how we should understand Revelation 1:6 and 5:10 which say the same thing. God has made believers 'to be a kingdom and priests to serve our God'. That is how we should understand Revelation 20:6 too: 'Blessed and holy are those who share in the first resurrection', a reference to being born again. The second death (hell) has no power over them. Rather, 'they will be priests of God and of Christ and will reign with him for a thousand years'. The thousand years is variously understood but we suggest that it is best understood as the whole period between the first and second comings of Christ.

If we read the Old Testament properly we will see that it is consistently moving in this direction. If you want to be biblical then keep in mind the priesthood of all believers.

It is a reminder that God must be worshipped and this can only be done through a priest

The Ten Commandments teach us that God must be worshipped and that he must be worshipped in the way that he lays down. Given the amount of material in Scripture that speaks of the need of an intermediary, a go-between, some sort of priest, it is pretty clear that in any true worship priesthood is going to be a vital issue.

In Exodus 33:20 God tells Moses, 'You cannot see my face, for no one may see me and live.' People suppose that they can simply look at God and speak to him, but it is clearly not that easy.

Looking at the sun in the sky sounds easy too but we know that if you want to do it for any length of time and survive you need to use a filter or some form of protection. With God also, some sort of intermediary is absolutely vital. We know that Jesus, the God-man, is the one Mediator between God and human beings and the only people who can come to him are true believers, who are all, men and women, their own priests.

It opposes all forms of sacerdotalism or priestcraft

Have you heard people say that they are against religion? Very often, if you scratch below the surface, what they are in fact against is priestcraft. They do not like the idea of a priest coming between a man and his God. The problem is an obvious one. If I am dependent on someone else to represent me before God then I am in a very vulnerable position. How easy for him to take advantage. Indeed, many would say all priests are taking advantage for there is no God and so there is no way to him, and so on.

Now the truth is that there is a God and that there is a way to him, but it is not through merely human priests but through the one true high priest, Jesus Christ. Each person must go himself to God through him and through him alone.

Roman Catholicism is an obvious example of where this is denied. 'You need a priest,' they say. 'You need a man who can bring you to God. He can baptise you as a baby and you can confess your sins to him. He can give you penance and absolve you of your sins. He can feed you on the body of Christ and he can give you the last rites and get you to the other side. He can pray for you when you are dead,' and so on. Now all this is very much against what the Bible actually teaches.

Priestcraft is not confined to Romanism either. There are so-called Protestants who think their ministers are like Roman priests. As a minister, I am often slightly nervous if a Christian asks me to pray for them. If they are seeking fellowship in prayer all very well but I do not want to encourage the idea that I necessarily have greater access to God than any other believer. Too many try to get their religion vicariously through their minister. There are too many ministers too who are willing to let them think like that.

And it is not just religious people who are sacerdotal either. The way some people treat scientists and other experts has all the marks of sacerdotalism. There is a growing willingness among some to trust what scientists and other professed experts say at face value and presume that they must be right. All we need to do is to listen to them, it is implied. Thankfully others exercise a healthy scepticism. The journalist Henry Gee has pointed out how scientists and those who pretend to be scientists 'cling to the mantle of a kind of religious authority'. When that happens, he says, 'there is no such thing as criticism. There is only blasphemy'.

The Bible brings us back to the need to take responsibility for ourselves. More will be said on this, but one of the great Protestant principles is the right of private interpretation. This means that no so called church or priest has the right to force an opinion on you. On the other hand, it does not mean that you just come up with your own ideas, regardless of others. No, we must weigh things up for ourselves and come to our own conclusions. We are responsible before God.

It means that every believer is close to God, not far off

Medieval Christianity taught that the church was part of a celestial hierarchy. Everything in heaven and on earth had its place in a great chain of being. At the top of the great chain was God, then came angels and archangels in heaven. The heavenly hierarchy was paralleled on earth by the sacraments which can only be understood by those God enables to comprehend and initiate them. God passes his knowledge and grace down the chain to the angels, then, and it is as the sacraments are administered by the priests, the clergy, that they are transferred to the people, the laity. Salvation, then, is chiefly through the sacraments and so via the priests, a unique class of people gifted by God to bring people to him. This view of a hierarchy prevailed in the church until the coming of the Protestant Reformation in the 16th century. Typically pithy, Luther once summed up: 'Faith alone is the true priestly office.'

For J. V. Fesko the most significant blessing that comes when we understand this is that there is no longer a hierarchy of beings standing between the believer and God—archangels, angels, archbishops, bishops, priests. Rather, believers have union and communion with God directly through our great high priest, Jesus Christ. When he died on the cross, the curtain in the Temple dividing the holy place and the most holy was torn from top to bottom, symbolising the fact that Christ had opened up a new and living way into God's immediate presence for all believers.

It is a reminder that every believer has a part to play in Christ's church

This is one of the most obvious things that comes out of this important teaching. If all believers are priests then all believers have a part to play.

You cannot just leave everything to the minister or to the paid staff, as some would like to do. No, every individual must play his part.

Take Ephesians 2:19–22 as an example of how the New Testament sees things:

…you are no longer foreigners and strangers, but fellow citizens with God's people and also members of his household, built on the foundation of the apostles and prophets, with Christ Jesus himself as the chief cornerstone. In him the whole building is joined together and rises to become a holy temple in the Lord. And in him you too are being built together to become a dwelling in which God lives by his Spirit.

Now there have been some who have taken this to extremes. Take the Plymouth Brethren for example. They tried to get rid of all ministers. It is an overreaction to clericalism and ultimately a mistake.

A BRIEF NOTE ON THE PLYMOUTH BRETHREN

The Brethren or Plymouth Brethren is the name used for a conservative, nonconformist, evangelical Christian movement whose history can be traced back to Dublin, Ireland, in the late 1820s, where it arose out of Anglicanism. A restorationist movement, it seeks to recapture the dynamics of the early church by means of an idiosyncratic interpretation and application of the Bible. The central figures early on were Anthony Norris Groves, a dentist studying theology at Trinity College; Edward Cronin, a medical student; John Nelson Darby, a curate in County Wicklow and John Gifford Bellett, a lawyer, who brought them together. They dispensed with ministers and liturgy to a great extent gathering around the Lord's Table Sunday morning by Sunday morning when men in the congregation would take turns to speak or exhort those gathered around the table. It was greatly influenced by the prophecy movement early on and has traditionally been dispensationalist and premillennialist in its eschatology.

Paul is clear in Ephesians 4:11–16:

Christ himself gave the apostles, the prophets, the evangelists, the pastors and teachers, to equip his people for works of service, so that the body of Christ may be built up until we all reach unity in the faith and in the knowledge of the Son of God and become mature, attaining to the whole measure of the fullness of Christ. Then we will no longer be infants, tossed back and forth by the waves, and blown here and there by every wind of teaching and by the cunning and craftiness of people in their deceitful scheming. Instead, speaking the truth in love, we will grow to become in every respect the mature body of him who is the head, that is, Christ. From him the whole body, joined and held together by every supporting ligament, grows and builds itself up in love, as each part does its work.

The whole body unites and works together as one priesthood, but different ones have different gifts and they must use them appropriately. In the Old Testament different Levites and priests were assigned different tasks. Some played music, some sang, some guarded the temple, others made sacrifices. We are not all preachers but we all have a part to play. Are you playing your part?

It puts right emphasis on everyday life rather than on mere public image

When we think about Christianity, there is a danger at times of merely focusing on the outward and the public—things like church gatherings for worship. Such matters are of great importance but they take up only a relatively small part of the life of the average Christian. For most Christians, more than 90% of their week is spent in activity that is not public worship.

A right emphasis on the priesthood of all believers is a great help here, therefore, as it reminds us of how important all of our activity is as Christians, whether it is done in public or in private, whether one is engaged in active worship or not.

It gives every believer a mandate to be a representative of Christ to the outsider

Timothy George has pointed out that Calvin interpreted the priesthood of all believers in terms of the church's participation in the threefold office of Christ as Prophet, King and Priest. This means that every Christian is mandated to represent Christ in his redemptive outreach to the world.

All believers ... should seek to bring others into the church, and should strive to lead the wanderers back to the road, should stretch forth a hand to the fallen and should win over the outsiders.

The priesthood of all believers is not something that encourages us to rest on our laurels but a commission that sends us out into the world to exercise a priestly ministry, not for ourselves but for others as yet outside the churches. It is to be done for the sake of Christ and because he has commanded us to go into all the world and preach the gospel in his name and on his behalf.

8. What further reasons are there why the priesthood of all believers matters?

'We are not to believe things in religion merely because they are said by Popes or Cardinals ... Bishops or Priests ... Puritans, or Reformers. We are not to argue, "Such and such things must be true—because these men say so." We are not to do so. We are to prove all things by the Word of God' (J. C. Ryle).

Therefore, I urge you, brothers and sisters, in view of God's mercy, to offer your bodies as a living sacrifice, holy and pleasing to God—this is your true and proper worship.

Romans 12:1

The Puritans were men who, it cannot be denied, knew how to preach. If you look at a Puritan sermon you will see that it closes with what are called 'uses'. Sometimes there are a large number of these. A Puritan preacher did not consider his sermon finished until he had applied his text. It was not enough merely to expound it and draw out the doctrine. The application may be by way of instruction or information, of confutation or exhortation or admonition. Sometimes it was intended to comfort or to aid in self-examination. Here is a good example. It is right not only to read about what the Bible says of the priesthood of all believers but to see the implications of that teaching too.

The priesthood of all believers is clearly taught in the New Testament. These final chapters look at why all this matters. A number of things are covered in the previous chapter, a further half dozen or so are matters that are covered in this chapter.

It puts a right emphasis on self-denial

Priests make sacrifices. We have spoken briefly about those sacrifices. 1 Peter 2:5 speaks in general terms of 'offering spiritual sacrifices acceptable to God through Jesus Christ'. As we have already noted previously, the rest of the New Testament specifies that these sacrifices include:

- *Faith* (Philippians 2:17): '... the sacrifice and service coming from your faith ...'

- *Praise* (Hebrews 13:15): 'Through Jesus, therefore, let us continually offer to God a sacrifice of praise—the fruit of lips that openly profess his name.'

- *Prayer* (Revelation 5 8) '... golden bowls full of incense, which are the prayers of God's people.'

- *Sharing with others* (Hebrews 13:16): 'And do not forget to do good and to share with others, for with such sacrifices God is pleased.' (Philippians 4:18) Paul says of the gifts the Philippians sent him 'They are a fragrant offering, an acceptable sacrifice, pleasing to God.'

- *All of life* (Romans 12:1): 'Therefore, I urge you, brothers and sisters, in view of God's mercy, to offer your bodies as a living sacrifice, holy and pleasing to God—this is your true and proper worship.'

The priesthood puts sacrifice at the heart of the Christian life. To be a true priest, there must be sacrifice and self-denial. Otherwise, we are not really living as priests.

If we want to think of a post-biblical example of sacrifice perhaps one of the greatest is found in the story of Henry Martyn.

Martyn studied in Cambridge University where he was an outstanding undergraduate scholar. He took the blue ribbon in a year of distinguished mathematicians, was Senior Wrangler in the class list and won the prestigious Smith's prize. He distinguished himself in classics too and became public examiner for the University when still barely out of his teens. After some uncertainty about where he stood in relation to Christ, he came under the influence of Charles Simeon and the 'Clapham Sect'. He resolved to abandon his enviable prospects in England and devote himself to overseas missionary work.

A BRIEF NOTE ON HENRY MARTYN

Henry Martyn (1781–1812) was a missionary to India and Iran. Born in Truro, Cornwall, he studied in St John's College, Cambridge, where he came under the spell of the influential Anglican evangelical preacher, Charles Simeon 1759–1836. Martyn went on to be a chaplain for the British East India Company, arriving in India in 1806. There he translated the New Testament into Urdu, into the Persian language and into Judaeo-Persic, a hybrid Persian and Hebrew language, widely spoken at the time. From India, Martyn set out for Iran but was seized with a fever and was forced to stop in Tokat, which today is in Turkey. There he died from tuberculosis, aged only 31. He is widely remembered for his courage, his selflessness and his Christian devotion. Several biographies about him exist. He once wrote these often quoted words: 'Let me burn out for God. After all, whatever God may appoint, prayer is the great thing. Oh, that I might be a man of prayer!'

About this time he became acquainted with Lydia Grenfell, with whom he fell in love. She was six years older but that was part of the attraction. As a youth he distrusted himself and yearned for a human prop on whom to lean. This comes out in his subsequent correspondence with her, after she decided not to marry him. When he fell in love with her he was unaware that she had been engaged to a man who proved so unworthy of her that the engagement was broken off. While this man remained unmarried, Lydia, while resolved never to marry him, considered herself morally bound not to marry anyone else.

This appears to have been a catalyst for her rejection of Martyn, whom she greatly admired. Though she broke off all correspondence with him for fear of growing too fond of him, hearing of his sister's death, she later wrote offering to renew correspondence. Her unworthy lover meanwhile married and her scruples were thus removed. Martyn accepted her offer with eagerness and gratitude and continued to write to her to the end on terms of most affectionate intimacy. However, by this time he had made up his mind to live a celibate life and never again to ask for her hand.

This element in Martyn's life is of immense human interest. At the same time it illustrates a rare spirit of self-sacrifice, one that distinguished his character. A young man of his ability and attainments could have had a lucrative and distinguished career in the University or at the Bar. He would have greatly increased his chances of winning Lydia's hand had he stayed in England. But he threw away all his prospects and subdued his desire to marry, believing God wanted him to preach the gospel in India. This conflict between desire and duty tormented him for years after leaving England and it was only on the strong recommendation of Simeon and others that late in the day he eventually wrote at last from India to ask Lydia to become his wife. She refused in light of the reason highlighted, her mother's unwillingness to give her consent and the even higher motive that marriage might lessen the love that she and Martyn had for God.

A lesser-known example of a life of sacrifice would be that of Allen Gardiner (1794–1851). Converted young, he first served in the navy, distinguishing himself across the world in war and peace. Long interested in pioneer missionary work, when one of his daughters tragically died, he decided to devote his remaining years to it.

At first he worked in South Africa but political events and native wars combined to prevent permanent success and he switched attention to South America. From 1838-1843, he laboured among indigenous peoples in Chile. He spent March, 1842, travelling from island to island in what is now Tierra del Fuego, his efforts hampered by opposition from various governments.

Having appealed to established societies to send missionaries to Patagonia without success in 1844 he was instrumental in forming the Patagonian Missionary Society. He and Robert Hunt, a schoolmaster, were the first missionaries. They were unable to establish a mission and returned home the following year.

Gardiner left England again, in September 1845, with his Spanish teacher Federico Gonzales, for Bolivia. There they distributed Bibles to indigenous peoples in the face of strong opposition from the Roman Catholic hierarchy. Having established Gonzales as a missionary at Potosi, Gardiner returned to England, reaching home by February, 1847.

The next year he returned to Tierra del Fuego, where he suffered great hardships, surveying the islands with a view to evangelisation. Having tried to interest others who could not help, he proposed establishing a mission using a substantial ship rather than being land based. When, at last, a lady from Cheltenham gave £700, a mission was determined on. In September, 1850, he sailed to the islands, accompanied by six others. They landed at Picton Island in December with two launches, each 26 feet long, stowed with six months worth of provisions. The climate was severe, the country barren and the native Yahgan people hostile. Six months elapsed without additional supplies, detained at the Falkland Islands for want of a vessel. The group ended up making the supreme sacrifice, gradually dying of starvation. Gardiner is believed to have survived longest, dying September 6, 1851.

On October 21 they were all found dead and on January 6, 1852, men from *HMS Dido* buried them. Gardiner's last journal entry simply said, 'I am overwhelmed with a sense of the goodness of God.' It should be added that two years later an 88-ton schooner *The Allen Gardiner* went to Patagonia as a British missionary ship and in 1856 his only son arrived to carry on the work his father began.

Sacrifice was at the heart of the lives of the Old Testament priests. It was at the heart of the lives of men like Martyn, Gardiner and other heroes of the faith. Is it at the heart of your life and mine?

It is a reminder that every believer must read, interpret and apply the Bible

Because all believers are priests, not just ministers, then, as noted, every believer has the right and authority to read, interpret and apply the teachings of the Bible. It is not reserved to priests or to a certain section of the church. We are no longer forced to rely on the church's interpretation. Like the Bereans in Paul's day we are rather to examine the Scriptures in order to know its teaching (Acts 17:11).

In practice this does not mean ignoring ministers or pretending they have nothing to teach us. Rather, it is a recognition that every person who is united to Christ by faith has a share in his priestly office. Ministers are gifts to the church given by Christ (Ephesians 4:11–12). They need the people and the people need them (1 Corinthians 12:4–26).

Some theologians get worried about the idea of private judgement and certainly some caution is necessary. Timothy George points out how some fall into the habit of talking about the 'priesthood of *the believer*' whereas the reformers always spoke of the 'priesthood of *all believers*' (plural). For them, he says, it was never a matter of a lonely, isolated seeker of truth but rather of a band of faithful believers united in a common confession as a local, visible congregation. He quotes Eastwood on the priesthood, the rhyming couplet we like to use to refer to the academic tome. A Methodist, Cyril Eastwood wrote a whole PhD on the subject of the priesthood of all believers. He laments distortions, which leads him to prefer not to identify the priesthood of believers with private judgement. He notes that for the reformers private judgement was always *informed* judgement:

...always controlled, checked, and corroborated by the testimony of the congregation. Indeed, Calvin himself fully realised that uncontrolled private judgment means subjectivism, eccentricity, anarchy, and chaos.

If we stick with Jim Packer (1926–2020) we will not go far wrong. He says:

All Christians have a right and duty not only to learn from the church's heritage of faith but also to interpret Scripture for themselves. The church of Rome doubts this, alleging that individuals easily misinterpret the Scriptures. This is true; but the following rules, faithfully observed, will help prevent that from happening...

He then sets out some obvious parameters: avoid allegorising; remember that the Bible is both a human composition and something we can understand only if God himself illumines our minds. The main thrust is always clear, he asserts:

...even if details are clouded. So when we understand the words used, the historical background, and the cultural conventions of the writer and his readers, we are well on the way to grasping the thoughts that are being conveyed.

However, we must pray that God's Spirit may generate the writer's passion in us and show us God in the text. If we remember the Bible's progressive nature, its unity, the need for Scripture to interpret Scripture and the importance of application, all will be well.

It is a reminder to every believer to pray

If a person is born again they have the privilege of going directly to God in prayer, without any earthly mediator. They are free to 'approach God's throne of grace with confidence, so that' they 'may receive mercy and find grace to help … in … time of need' (Hebrews 4:16).

Such prayer is personal and real. The sinner comes before the sovereign God, who knows the secrets of our hearts, with genuine repentance. Such prayer includes confession. Private sins are to be privately confessed, public sins in public. Confession is followed by forgiveness, peace of conscience and a fresh start.

Prayer is also to be earnest (see James 5:16). We are to ask, confident that it will be given. We are to intercede from the heart. Such prayers are not likely to be liturgical or read prayers.

No human mediator is required between God's people and their Lord. To pray in Jesus' name is enough. In a short article on the subject Ian MacNaughton has written rightly:

In this New Testament era, the throne of grace is ever open to all who come in faith to God, through Christ, exercising the gift of prayer. It is guaranteed that they will be welcomed by the Lord.

It is a reminder of what an honour it is to be a Christian

Thomas Manton wrote of this matter:

Now this is a great honour, that we should be separated by the Lord from all the rest of the world, and admitted into such a nearness and access to God with boldness, and hope of being accepted through Christ.

He says that it is a reason to give continual praise and glory to Christ. What a tremendous privilege—to be a priest to God.

It puts an end to the idea of dividing life up between sacred and secular

Some people try to divide their lives into secular and sacred. So, for example, going to church is obviously sacred and so going to school or work must be secular. Reading the Bible is sacred but reading the newspaper is secular. Communion is sacred but having a meal at a restaurant is secular. Praying is sacred but watching TV is secular. Witnessing is sacred and talking about football is secular, etc., etc.

That way of dividing up your life is completely unbiblical. Rather, we are instructed in 1 Corinthians 10:31, 'whether you eat or drink or whatever you do, do it all for the glory of God', and in Colossians 3:17 it says, 'And whatever you do, whether in word or deed, do it all in the name of the Lord Jesus, giving thanks to God the Father through him.'

If we remember that we are priests to God, it will be a great help to us in that direction. Whatever I do, I must do it in a holy and God-honouring way, as a priest to God.

It exalts Christ to his rightful place

A proper understanding of the priesthood of all believers will almost inevitably lead to a higher view of Christ. Instead of thinking that some human being can be our means to heaven we will see that Christ alone can do it. He alone is our High Priest. Hebrews 7:23–28:

Now there have been many of those [Old Testament] priests, since death prevented them from continuing in office; but because Jesus lives forever, he has a permanent priesthood. Therefore he is able to save completely those who come to God through him, because he always lives to intercede for them. Such a high priest truly meets our need—one who is holy, blameless, pure, set apart from sinners, exalted above the heavens. Unlike the other high priests, he does not need to offer sacrifices day after day, first for his own sins, and then for the sins of the people. He sacrificed for their sins once for all when he offered himself. For the law appoints as high priests men in all their weakness; but the oath, which came after the law, appointed the Son, who has been made perfect forever.

J. V. Fesko says helpfully:

Rejoice that because of your union with Christ you share in all who he is and does. In this case, his high priestly office means that you too are a holy and royal priest.

It is a spur to godliness and a great encouragement in the Christian life

I am a Christian minister. From time to time I find myself meeting strangers. Often one of the first things I am asked about is what I do. The moment I say that I am a preacher, as you may imagine, there is some level of reaction. People expect certain things from ministers. These do not always fit tightly with what the Bible would teach but there is a broad correlation.

Now, in a similar way, if people know that we are priests to God then it is bound to encourage us in the right direction. I am not suggesting that you tell people that you are a priest in most cases, but if you live as a New Testament priest ought to live then you will inevitably be led into godly ways.

Perhaps we can add what an encouraging thing it is to realise that you are a priest of God. It is a great thing to be set aside in this way and to know that your whole life belongs to the Lord.

It is the root of more general ideas of equality in society

Perhaps we can add one more thing, something briefly highlighted in the 19th century by Bishop Lightfoot. He wrote:

It will hardly be denied, I think, by those who have studied the history of modern civilization with attention, that this conception of the Christian Church has been mainly instrumental in the emancipation of the degraded and oppressed, in the removal of artificial barriers between class and class, and in the diffusion of a general philanthropy, untrammelled by the fetters of party or of race; in short, that to it mainly must be attributed the most important advantages which constitute the superiority of modern societies over ancient. Consciously or unconsciously, the idea of a universal priesthood, of the religious equality of all men, which, though not untaught before, was first embodied in the Church of Christ, has worked, and is working, untold blessings in political institutions, and in social life.

Of course, the idea has not been fully understood or implemented in the church, let alone in society. Nevertheless, the very thing that modern democracies at their best appear to be striving for is found embodied in New Testament teaching and practice. When old fashioned trade unionists and other political movements speak of one another as brothers and sisters, it is clear they are speaking in terms borrowed from the Bible.

***

So those are six further reasons why the priesthood of all believers is such an important truth. We must continue to see this truth in Scripture and think about it and live it out with God's help.

9. Our work as priests in the new heavens and the new earth

'Here we do but tune our instruments, and prepare for the work of Heaven, but then we perform it … to be Kings and Priests unto God, doth not respect the present life only but our ministration in the heavenly Temple. There is a for ever, always affixed to the doxologies of the saints; to show that now they do but begin in the Work, which they shall complete hereafter' (Thomas Manton).

…and from Jesus Christ, who is the faithful witness, the firstborn from the dead, and the ruler of the kings of the earth. To him who loves us and has freed us from our sins by his blood, and has made us to be a kingdom and priests to serve his God and Father—to him be glory and power for ever and ever! Amen.

Revelation 1:5–6

In the second of two sermons on Revelation 1:5–6, Thomas Manton takes up the subject 'our priesthood, when we shall be admitted into the immediate presence of God, and praise him for evermore'. He reminds us that, in this life, believers minister before the throne of grace, but in the world to come they will minister before the throne of glory. As he comments, 'it is a truth commonly overlooked' but one that is very important. It is an appropriate one with which to end this brief study of the priesthood of all believers.

Manton uses several arguments to show that part of our heavenly existence will consist of serving God as his priests.

Revelation 7:14–16

Manton draws attention to Revelation 7:14–16 which explicitly speaks of the time when believers have come out of their great tribulation, having washed their robes and made them white in Christ's blood. It says:

Therefore, they are before the throne of God and serve him day and night in his temple; and he who sits on the throne will shelter them with his presence.

It is an explicit statement of priestly activity in heaven, an activity that is constant. Under the law, the Levitical priests served God day and night by working in shifts. That is replicated today to some extent by the fact that the church of God is a worldwide phenomenon. When one part of the church is sleeping, the other part is able to worship. In the eloquent words of John Ellerton (1801–1873):

As over continent and island
each dawn leads on another day,
the voice of prayer is never silent,
nor do the praises die away.

In that day, however, there will literally be worship at all times from every believer. They will never tire and there will be no sin and as God is always present they will cheerfully serve him always.

Kings and priests

Given that believers are made kings as well as priests and that their kingship is chiefly something that lies in the future, it is reasonable to suppose that much of our work as priests also lies in the future. Here on earth we reign only in a spiritual way. It is only in heaven that we will tread Satan under our feet, triumph over our enemies and reign visibly. Then we will judge angels and our kingship will continue through eternity.

In a similar way, we are spiritual priests here on earth, our sacrifices consisting chiefly of prayers, praises, gifts and devotion to the Lord. When we are in heaven, however, we will be in the Holiest place of all, not just in spirit but in person.

It is part of our conformity to Christ

Christ must have the pre-eminence in all things (Colossians 1:8) but those God foreknew, he predestined to be conformed to the image of his Son, that he might be the first-born among many brothers (Romans 8:29). Now it was in his death and what followed that Christ's priesthood chiefly consists. His great sacrifice occurred on the cross and his work of intercession begins in earnest only when he ascends to heaven. Given that Christ is a pattern to which believers must be conformed, it is no surprise if the chief part of their priesthood begins also at death.

Heaven a Temple

The Old Testament Temple was a type not only of Christ and of the church but also of heaven. Heaven can be thought of as a Temple. If it is a temple, then it is appropriate that there should be priests and worship there. Manton suggests that as the Temple had an outward court, a holy place and the holiest place of all, so we have three heavens above us—the sky, the stars and the heaven of heavens, the third heaven where God's throne of glory is and where God's people dwell and where they will worship and serve him continually.

Heaven an eternal Sabbath

In Hebrews 4:9 the writer speaks of a rest that remains for the people of God, a Sabbath rest. A Sabbath is a day for holy rest not for idleness. Given that there is a glorious eternal rest prepared for believers and promised to them, we can expect in heaven not a time of idleness but of worship and adoration. 'It is a rest from toil and labour, but not from work and service', notes Manton. Under the Law, the sacrifices were doubled on the Sabbath not reduced. The priests had more to do that day than any other. The Sabbath is to be a delight, a day given to God, and heaven will be that supremely and so will be marked by our delighting ourselves in God's presence by serving him as priests.

A BRIEF NOTE ON THE PURITAN THOMAS MANTON

Thomas Manton was an English Puritan and a Presbyterian. In his time, he was one of three clerks or secretaries to the Westminster Assembly, a chaplain to Oliver Cromwell and preached before Parliament at least six times. Born in Somerset and educated at Oxford, he went on to serve briefly in Sowton and Colyton in Devon, 1640–1645, before moving on to minister in Stoke Newington, until 1656, then just outside London and Covent Garden, until 1662. At the Restoration, Manton was on favourable terms with Charles II and was offered the Deanery of Rochester but refused it on conscientious grounds and was ejected with hundreds of others. He continued to preach and write as he could and in 1670 was arrested and imprisoned for six months. He became a lecturer at Pinner's Hall where the 'morning exercises' were delivered. Forgotten today, he was held in high esteem in his day by men like John Owen. He was best known for his skilled expository preaching and in the nineteenth century, thanks to men like Ryle and Spurgeon, his *Works* were republished in 22 volumes. Spurgeon says they contain 'a mighty mountain of sound theology' and are 'second to none'. For him, 'Manton is not brilliant, but he is always clear; he is not oratorical, but he is powerful; he is not striking, but he is deep.'

Praise and thanksgiving will go on forever

It has been noted that as priests, believers offer sacrifices in thanksgiving and praise rather than as a means of atonement. There is no reason to suppose that thanksgiving and praise will cease in heaven. Quite the opposite. It will go on forever. Manton says:

We shall then have a fuller sense of the mercies and goodness of God, when our redemption is full and complete, and a clearer sight of his excellencies when we see him face to face. Here we do but tune our instruments, and prepare for the work of heaven, but then we perform it.

Here on earth we are learning to praise God. We do it by faith. When we use the word *forever* in connection with praise, as in the phrase 'Yours be the glory forever and ever', it is a reminder of this fact. Here on earth worship is just beginning.

It is only then that believers will be fully qualified and prepared

Here on earth believers are justified and progressively sanctified. Only at death will they be fully sanctified and fully ready to be consecrated as heavenly priests. Just as the Levitical priests were consecrated over a seven day period before ministering, so believers are being consecrated here on earth for the work of serving that will begin in heaven. Only then will they be fully ready to approach the throne of glory.

Lessons

So a chief part of the priesthood of the believer lies in the future, when Christ comes and the kingdom is fully established. Of what use is such knowledge today? Manton ends his sermon with a number of uses or applications.

He makes three sorts of application—informational, exhortational and by way of comfort.

INFORMATION

As for information, two things. First, this is a reminder that to worship God is a privilege. Our work in heaven, which will be worship, is a part of our reward. There is no greater privilege on earth than to be serving God. Nothing that the men and women of this world do begins to compare with this amazing privilege. Believers have begun on a wonderful work in this life that will go on forever.

Secondly, it is no easy matter to be familiar with God and to draw near him in worship. By nature we are rather stupid and do not realise this but reverence is essential in such matters. 'In the council of the holy ones God is greatly feared; he is more awesome than all who surround him' (Psalm 89:7). We are to come to God boldly but also with a humble sense of privilege. In the Old Testament the priests were more qualified to draw near to God and be employed in his most holy service than the common people. Believers today are separated from the world in order to come near to God. It is no easy matter to come before him as we ought to, however, and we should be very thankful for the honour of serving him imperfectly now and without sin in the world to come.

EXHORTATION

Two things again. Firstly, if you are a believer, you should be longing for the time when you will minister in heaven. When you are fully sanctified, you will be admitted to that blessed estate.

On that day, you will see the one you worship and stand before his throne.

When he shall appear we shall be like him, for we shall see him as he is (1 John 3:2).

Father, I want those you have given me to be with me where I am, and to see my glory, the glory you have given me because you loved me before the creation of the world (John 17:24).

What a blessing to see what you love and to possess what you see. Here we worship God as an unseen God. He is not unknown but he is unseen. There, he will be known and seen. There vision succeeds faith, hope comes to fruition and perfect love reigns. Manton reminds us that 'The immediate presence of God, which is our felicity in heaven, would be our misery upon earth.' No one on earth can see him and live (Exodus 33:20). Just as you cannot look at the sun without losing your eyesight, so you cannot look at God now, but then our souls and bodies will be ready to see him.

On that day, the believer will serve him perfectly without weakness, weariness or wandering thoughts. Our ideas of God are dull and low. How irreverent and inadequate our praise. The best of God's servants if they see a little of his glory, are greatly humbled. When we see him as he is, then we will better praise him, and have more noble thoughts of him. Now we cannot endure praising him for long, but there communion with God will be ever new and fresh to us every moment. The angels never weary of looking at God and enjoying his glorious presence. One day we will be the same. Further, here on earth we are often and easily distracted, but in heaven there will be nothing to divert us from thinking of God. What a comfort in our present weakness and weariness to know that!

On that day we will serve God without interruption. There will be no impediments; no need of sleep, for example. We will always stand before his throne of glory and remain in his wonderful presence. We will need no rest and there will be no night. No miseries will distract us either. Christ will be with us and we will be with him.

On that day we will enter into a closer communion with God than we have ever known. We draw near to him now but in heaven all distance will be gone. We will know immediate and full fellowship. Here we only get glimpses of him, though the more we draw near, the more like him we become. In heaven we will be so near him, we will be just like him (1 John 3:2).

Another feature of the coming day will be the complete unity of God's people at that time. We are urged to unity now but we often fail to be united. Then, there will be perfect unity and complete harmony.

On that day believers will entirely be taken up with the worship of God. Just as the angels praise him without stint, so will they and with even more reason, given the great salvation that they have received.

Secondly, this fact should induce believers to prepare themselves for what is to come. We ought to be living in a way consistent with this glorious future. In particular, there should be an increasing desire for holiness. 'Blessed are the pure in heart, for they will see God' (Matthew 5:8). The more we cleanse ourselves from filthiness, the more of God we will see. Manton says:

Let us begin our sacrifices, and discharge our priestly office now, and perform all the duties which belong to our ministration with more fidelity.

Some duties are proper only to the present state, but 'none are priests in heaven but those that have acted the priest's part upon earth'. Other duties will go on beyond the grave, and praise is one of them. It must begin now.

The thought of heaven should also make us eager to be more frequently with God. Surely, says Manton, that life on earth is best that is most like the life of heaven and so worship should loom large in our thinking. Prayer makes us more familiar with God than anything else on earth can. It is the best way to prepare for 'entrance upon our everlasting priesthood'. Who would try swimming in an ocean before he has swum in brooks and streams? 'Communion with God in a way of grace is the way to communion with him in a way of glory.' Seeing him now with the eye of faith is the best preparation for seeing God face to face in the world to come.

A final thing by way of exhortation is to call on us to be more aware of what a privilege it is to come near to God. On one hand, we should be ashamed that we are so slow to draw near to God and how weary we can become of serving the Lord. On the other, we should thankful that we have been redeemed by Christ and can so confidently go into his presence even now (see Ephesians 3:12; Hebrews 4:16).

COMFORT

Though we can be very poor at worshipping today, one day we shall express our thanksgiving to God perfectly. We must not be discouraged by present troubles and sufferings.

This truth should also make us willing to die if we are believers, as then we will serve the Lord in heaven as his priests. David longed for the enjoyment of God in the earthly temple (Psalm 63). How much more ought we to long for the time when we will be made priests to him forever?

***

We close with the words of Isaac Watts:

> Now to the Lord, that makes us know
> The wonders of his dying love,
> Be humble honours paid below,
> And strains of nobler praise above.

'Twas he that cleansed our foulest sins,
And washed us in his richest blood;
'Tis He that makes us priests and
    kings,
And brings us rebels near to God.

To Jesus, our atoning priest,
To Jesus, our superior king,
Be everlasting power confessed,
And every tongue his glory sing.

Behold, on flying clouds he comes,
And every eye shall see him move;
Though with our sins we pierced
    him once,
Then he displays his pardoning love.

The unbelieving world shall wail,
While we rejoice to see the day:
Come, Lord; nor let thy promise fail,
Nor let thy chariots long delay.